Moving?
Saying Goodbye and
Saying Hello

Lois B. Hart, Ed.D.

Published by: HRD Press, Inc.
               22 Amherst Road
               Amherst, MA 01002
               800-822-2801 (U.S. and Canada)
               413-253-3488
               413-253-3490 (fax)

ISBN: 978-1-61014-435-3

Editorial services by Rachel Carkhuff
Production services by Jean S. Miller

Table of Contents

Table of Contents

Preface

When you think of moving, where does your mind go? Do you feel moving can be a blessing or a burden? A crisis or an opportunity? A memorable or miserable experience. Many of those who have moved innumerable times might tell you that they have experienced quite a range of feelings. It is both feelings about moving and thinking about the process of moving itself that I will be discussing with you.

Long ago, over time and over several moves, I learned the mechanics of moving. I made checklists of tasks to follow and created floor plans for the placement of the furniture in our new home. These tools have helped tremendously throughout the many moves I've made with my family.

It was over 47 years ago when my partner and I got married. We moved into a university dorm where he was the dorm director Then we moved to a condo near our kids' school and their grandparents. Next, we made a move to another state so I could get my advanced degree. I will never forget that after that move, it took about six months for the phone to ring! It took that long to greet, evaluate, and follow up with the new people I was meeting and to cement the relationships enough so there was a reason to call one another.

When faced with a move to yet another state for our new jobs, I knew I had to do something different this time—and I did! It wasn't the process of moving that was bogging me down; I had checklists, floor plans, and the like. It was the feelings about who I was leaving and who I would meet that kept me thinking. I wanted to be excited about new challenges and opportunities, but I didn't want to move forward if I was leaving established relationships with friends and colleagues behind.

The next cross-country move was to Colorado because we wanted a new climate, lifestyle and adventure. By now I'd learned networking skills that accelerated the success of my business by finding and establishing both personal and professional relationships. I had quite a few new people who called me, both sooner and more often than with previous moves. Within Colorado we moved to three other locations to be closer to work and the airport, and to build two homes.

Moving? Saying Goodbye and Saying Hello!

After 27 years in Colorado, our lives changed yet again! A life-threatening event shifted our view of our mortality. While vacationing in Montana, we decided to pursue another new adventure. We listed our reasons to move, found a new house, put ours on the market, and cleaned out the old and useless stuff. Again, I shifted to logistics first.

Then, my feelings made themselves known. Suddenly it occurred to us that a 1,000-mile move would definitely impact our relationships in Colorado and leave us friendless in Montana. I worried about how I could smoothly establish new personal friendships and find compatible professional colleagues. Fortunately, all went well and we weren't alone for long.

To further complicate our relationships and our feelings about those relationships, four years later we purchased a second home in Page, Arizona and have lived there for three winters. Now we had family and friends in three locations, each over 1,000 miles apart. That was a lot to juggle.

After nine years in Montana, we moved back to Colorado to be near our family, long-time friends, and better medical care. We chose a different part of the state so once again, we started over. As I write this story of our moving history, in 2017, we have moved to a nearby city that is not too far away from friends but, from our point of view, requires adding new people to our lives.

This is our 18th move over 47 years of marriage. Most people think we are eccentric, but every move has truly enhanced our lives, as we've had great adventures along the way.

I looked hard for a book on moving that covered the impact moving has on personal relationships. When I couldn't find one, *Moving? Saying Goodbye and Saying Hello!* was born.

This book is a compilation of everything I learned about how to make my phone ring wherever I lived. So, start packing and come along with me on this unique journey. You will start your journey by reviewing your moving history, learning about four phases of a *Moving Transition Model*, and identify your *Moving Style* and its impact as to how you approach moving.

Preface

You will take the trail to catalog your current relationships and evaluate who to drop and who to keep. You will explore the special qualities of your "Keepers" and develop a plan for staying in touch. Next you will learn how to say goodbye to those you will leave behind. Your last trail will explore techniques and strategies so you can choose the best people for your new network.

Bon Voyage!

Lois B. Hart, Ed.D.
Loveland, CO

Chapter 1

Move and Thrive!

Relocating to a new home and job can cause a Break Down or a Break Out for many of us. On a well-known test that lists events in our lives and ranks them as to the stress each one causes, moving and relocating is right up next to death and divorce.

The physical act of packing and moving stuff is a breakdown; possessions are removed from a familiar place and brought to an unknown space. When we change our physical location or space, we change our perspective as well. When all of our stuff shows up in new quarters, it has to be re-arranged to fit the specific spaces and may be used for different functions than before.

Moving can be transformative. If you are like the people I surveyed and interviewed about their past moves, you may not realize just how transformational a move can be for your life until you experience it.

Move and you can change your life. You change your place and you change your perspective. Changing your perspective includes attitudes, beliefs, hopes, dreams, and values. You will be transformed! When you move, you leave behind people and find new friends.

Every future move or relocation can be as positive a transformation as you make it. Even a move forced by adversity can be turned around into something beneficial.

Susan had been dreaming about a move to Colorado for several years, but personal circumstances kept her in California. We often teach what we need to learn and that is what happened in Susan's case. During this period, she developed and facilitated a personal transformation program. As she helped others work through a transformational model, this process naturally changed her readiness to try something new. Two years later, a love relationship ended, freeing her to move. She moved with both a new attitude and a new level of confidence. Susan recommends that if you have sufficient lead time before a move, read some books and/or take a workshop on transition and transformation.

Adversity can hasten a transformation. We have seen and read stories about people who overcame the most unimaginable challenges. How would you handle the loss of your home and everything you own, as so many did during the Katrina and Sandy hurricanes?

I met Lisa when she came to give an estimate for moving our possessions. Her southern accent and friendliness prompted me to ask where she was from and she said New Orleans. In the St. Bernard Parish, she and other family members lost three houses and only saved what they could fit into their cars. They experienced symptoms of Post-Traumatic Stress.

Lisa remembers that her mother once said she wanted to visit Boulder, Colorado someday. Lisa took this as a sign that she and her mother should move there. They drove to a new state, knowing no one, and with no jobs.

With some help from FEMA, the Red Cross, and a local church, Lisa got housing, a pre-school for her son, and a job. She created a new network in Colorado, starting with her colleagues and parents at her son's school. Lisa believed that moving to a new place would help them heal. Her bold plan and courage paid off.

Ken moved to Colorado for health reasons; he is now a vigorous and active 55-year-old. Karen followed her husband to Kansas City and turned her painful adjustment period into a new job. She holds workshops for other Trailing Spouses. Anne struggled with changes in her new location and used the opportunity to return to college to finish her degree.

Moving can result in other benefits too. Why not think about:

- Trying out new adventures in a new location?

- Making a fresh start with new people who truly share your values and beliefs?

- Joining others who share your talents like making jewelry, pottery, and crafts?

- Changing your exercise and eating lifestyle?

- Living in an intentional community—a community designed from the start to have a high degree of social cohesion and teamwork?

- Joining a new faith community?

- Starting a new business or a different role in your profession or career?

Moving? Saying Goodbye and Saying Hello is your guide for a successful moving journey. I suggest you read the book from the beginning to provide an important foundation. With an open mind, you can experience anything—at least once! You are bound to learn more about yourself and grow as a person. Life is a wonderful journey, full of the unexpected. Your move may, and can, end up changing your life. It is often a question of your choices.

Throughout this book, you will have many opportunities to respond to questions, record your thoughts and feelings, choose strategies for optimizing your transitional experiences, and record your progress on this particular life transformation—moving out—then moving on!

Chapter 2

What's Your Moving History?

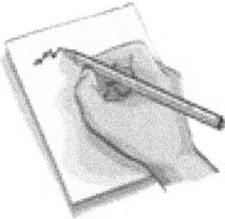

You just learned some of the reasons I've moved. What about you? Here are some questions about your previous moving experiences. Record your answers below. Answering these questions will help you to identify how you felt and its impact on future moves.

1. When was your last move? Was it during the last few years or at least a decade ago?

_____

_____

_____

2. Did you move across the city, to a new county, or even a new country?

_____

_____

_____

In the space below list all of the times you've moved, including when you were a child. Leave space between each to add notes to further questions.

First move:

_____

_____

_____

_____

_____

_____

Second move:

_____

_____

_____

_____

_____

Third move:

_____

_____

_____

_____

_____

Fourth move:

_____

_____

_____

_____

_____

Fifth move:

_____

_____

_____

_____

_____

Sixth move:

_____

_____

_____

_____

_____

_____

Other moves:

_____

_____

_____

_____

_____

Next, evaluate each of the moves on your list using the questions below. Use the space under each move to make your notes.

How did you feel about each of these moves? Were they happy or sad occasions, adventuresome or miserable?

Answers to these questions can determine how you will deal with your next moving experience.

Some people who move a lot are less daunted with the prospect of packing up again. I'm one of them. I lived in the same house until I went away to college. Early moves were caused by unfortunate situations, marrying young, and eventually divorcing. Once I married my second husband, who lived in lots of places during his time with the Air Force, we began a pattern of feeling very good about moving. To us, moving is a grand adventure! The shortest time we lived in one place was one year and the longest was 10 years, but we still have happy memories of every one of them.

Nancy moved 10 times as a child because she was a military "brat" (the military moves people about 10 times over a 20-year career). Her childhood moving experiences were mostly positive for two reasons. First, her parents had a stable marriage and a positive attitude towards the migratory military life. Second, the military provided a ready-made community for its families. She could live and go to school right on the base. The other children and adults greeted her with open arms and totally understood how she felt about leaving friends and starting over.

Since Nancy and I both had positive experiences when we moved, we both see today's moves as opportunities. We are excited about new communities, a new home, and new relationships.

There are many people who also moved a number of times, but now have the opposite attitude towards moving. Michael grew up so poor that his family was forced to move often when his parents continuously lost jobs and couldn't afford the rent. Sam had parents who had wanderlust; as a result, he attended 12 different schools in 15 years. Both hated the moment when they had to enter another classroom of strangers. They remember how hard it was to make new friends and how sad they were when they left good friends behind. Today they look upon relocating with anxiety and dread.

Who Moves and Why

The United States Census Bureau updates data on mobility on a yearly basis. The data is the latest available at the time of the publication of this book. Visit their website at census.gov for more data and updates.

The 2017 report confirms that 35.8 million people or 11% of the population moved. It includes information on the reasons people move.

Who moves the most?

- More single people than married couples
- More employed than unemployed people
- People with higher levels of education (associate degree and higher)

The top three by age who move are ages:

- 45–64 years
- 30–44 years
- 65–74 years

Work and Jobs

Sixteen percent of all people who move do so for various reasons, including to begin a new job, transfer to a new location, be closer to work, or to have an easier commute.

Housing

Twenty-seven percent of people move for a newer or better house, to a better neighborhood with less crime, for cheaper housing, because of a foreclosure or eviction, or they want to own a house and not rent anymore.

How Far People Move

Of people who moved, 6.8% did so within their own county. Those moving up to 50 miles were mostly changing their housing rather than because of jobs. People who moved over 50 miles impacted their relationships more.

Fifteen percent of people moved 200 to 499 miles, and 25% moved over 500 miles.

People with advanced degrees moved the farthest, primarily for job-related reasons. People who complete higher education seek jobs that use their knowledge and training. Many career-oriented people have a higher comfort level or tolerance for changing jobs and even more comfort in changing careers that require relocation.

Other Reasons People Move

Other reasons people move include:

- To establish their own household – 11.5%
- For other family reasons – 11%
- A change in marital status – 5.1%
- To attend college – 3%
- For their health – 2%
- For a better climate or location – 5%
- Because of natural disasters – 3%

Happy and Sad Reasons You Have Moved

Here is an expanded list of why people move for both positive and negative reasons. Read these lists and check those reasons or conditions that fit why you moved (or are moving), beginning at the age of 18 until today. Put the corresponding number from your moving history list next to the reasons.

Housing Related

- ❑ From renting to first ownership _____
- ❑ Want new or better housing _____
- ❑ Want better neighborhood _____
- ❑ Cheaper housing _____
- ❑ Foreclosure _____
- ❑ Eviction _____

Family Related

- ❑ Change in marital status _____
- ❑ Establish own household _____
- ❑ Help aging parents _____

Job Related

- ❏ New job _____
- ❏ Job transfer _____
- ❏ Lost job _____
- ❏ Looking for work _____
- ❏ Get closer to work _____
- ❏ Retired _____

Other

- ❏ Attend or leave college _____
- ❏ Change of climate _____
- ❏ Health reasons _____
- ❏ Disaster: fire, flood, earthquake, _____
  tornado, etc.

Look for patterns in your moving history.

1. Which of your reasons for moving happened the most?

_____
_____
_____
_____
_____

2. Did more positive or negative circumstances prompt your moves?

_____
_____
_____
_____

3. What surprised you from this review of your history?

_____

_____

_____

_____

_____

_____

_____

_____

_____

_____

When You Move, Your Relationships Change

No matter why you move or how far you move, your relationships will change. With every move, you will leave people behind. You will have to find ways to stay in touch with your "Keepers" (who you will read about in Chapter 5). At every new job, you will have new colleagues and/or clients. At your new home in a new neighborhood, you will have new neighbors.

Transition is not easy. It takes a concerted effort to build your network in a new location. Use what you learned from previous moves that may have been hard on you and change your perspective about moving so you will have a positive, transformational experience with every move.

Chapter 3

Four-Phase Moving Model

Some People Hate Moving!

In Chapter 2, you read about people who had such bad experiences moving that now they dreaded the idea of moving again.

People who dread moving may say:

- "I never want to move again!"
- "I hate change."
- "I'm dreading this move. I have such a hard time making new friends."
- "My life is over if I have to move to _____ (city or state)."
- "I hate to leave my best friends."
- "I'll never have a house as nice as this one!"
- "I'm going to be miserable."

Yes, the logistics of moving are difficult and seemingly endless, plus you will leave behind people you care about. This book will help you learn how to mitigate those negative experiences and create a more positive one. This chapter will provide a useful overview of what to expect on this journey.

A Four-Phase Moving Model

There are four predictable phases you will go through during the transition of moving.

The *Four-Phase Moving Model* describes what you can expect when you move:

Phase 1: Think about Moving

↓

Phase 2: Decide to Move

↓

Phase 3: Plan the Move

↓

Phase 4: Implement the Move

During each of the four phases, you will learn what people think about when moving; typical feelings that arise, and the implications on their jobs, housing, and especially on their relationships. Specific strategies are suggested to help resolve negative impacts on your friends, family, and colleagues.

As you read about these four phases, reflect upon your previous moves and compare your experiences with those of others.

Phase 1—Think about Moving

What to Expect

Phase 1 occurs when people are just thinking or considering the possibility of moving. This phase definitely feels like a prelude to something else happening. It is like being in limbo, set between today and the future. Some dream about a new place they've read about or perhaps visited. This dream might ultimately become the move!

People who have been laid off or fired from their jobs may think about a new job elsewhere; in a different organization located farther away from home. Other people who are bored with what they have been doing or need or want a change will often muse about a new or better opportunity in a different location. Other people are offered a promotion in another location.

Housing circumstances get people thinking about a move. Some people need to change the size of their home—bigger if the family size has increased or smaller after the kids have moved out. Many think it is time to stop renting and become homeowners. Some homeowners get to thinking about building a house to fulfill everything they want in their dream home. Business owners might need space for expanding their business.

Location is also a reason people move. The climate where they currently live might be too hot or cold, too humid or dry, too windy, too cloudy or foggy, or too sunny. The area might be prone to tornadoes, earthquakes, forest fires, or hurricanes; be too flat or mountainous; or have too many bugs or dangerous animals.

Others desire a move near specific geographic features such as rivers or lakes, mountains or plains. Some people want either a more or less quiet location. Yet others think about the pros and cons of living in rural, urban, or suburban areas, or even relocating to a foreign country. They may want to be closer to a job, cultural opportunities and events, recreational opportunities, or educational institutions.

Changes in health can also get people thinking about moving. They might need a different climate that will mitigate a health condition like asthma or heart disease. They may need to move closer to specific medical care. Caretakers of elderly parents think about moving closer to them because of their failing health. Many people move to support a healthier life style.

Another group of people may want to have a closer-knit community like a planned church or spiritual 'community", a "new town" or "new urbanism" community, a senior continuum of care residence, or a smaller town. They think about these options in order to have new and meaningful relationships.

People may want or need to be closer to relatives, to a new love relationship, or to special friends. The opposite might be considered too; to move away from certain relatives, a broken love relationship, or from a group of people with whom they've had negative experiences. During this thinking phase, the impact on current relationships is usually considered. People often share their thoughts with family or friends and say, "I'm thinking about moving to...."

During Phase 1, *Thinking about Moving,* you can expect to have feelings about the people in your life and their reactions to your news. You could feel uncertain, bewildered, confused, and fearful of the unknown. Or, you could approach the move with a sense of excitement and adventure.

You might have mixed feelings just thinking about a move, no less acting on the idea, because you recognize that you will leave special people behind. Some of your friends, family, and colleagues will try to dissuade you from going beyond the Thinking phase. Others will be helpful, encouraging you in the Thinking phase by asking clarifying questions or helping you brainstorm options and solutions to any issues you may have.

Strategies for Thinking about Moving

Some strategies for thinking about moving are:

- Consider reading a book on transition and personal change so you will understand what to expect.

- Talk with people who have moved successfully, and especially those who had positive experiences. Ask how they kept in touch with their friends and family and also how they found new relationships after the move.

- Make notes to identify what you are thinking, feeling, and talking about with others:

    ✓ "What do I really want and need?"

    _____

    _____

    _____

    _____

    _____

✓ "What changes would I like to make in my life?"

_____

_____

_____

_____

_____

- Record and rank your reasons for moving now compared to your previous moves.

Ranking	Reasons for Moving
_____	_____
_____	_____
_____	_____
_____	_____
_____	_____
_____	_____

- Note potential rewards and costs to you and/or your family if you choose to make this move. Perhaps the move is not your choice. In this case, jot down ideas of what you could do to reduce the negative impacts on your life.

_____

_____

_____

_____

_____

- Visualize yourself in the potential locations you might choose. Add scenes of positive things happening, including new friends and colleagues. Pay attention to how this makes you feel.

_____

_____

_____

_____

_____

Phase 2—Decide to Move

What to Expect

Phase 2 begins when people go beyond simply thinking about moving to making the decision to actually move. They are ready to announce their decision to others and to start facing the realities of moving. This phase still feels like limbo because although the major decision to move is made, there are so many additional decisions to make. These decisions include:

- **Employment**—do you have a job lined up, or will you begin your job hunt after the move?

- **Housing**—will you rent, buy, or build a house? What kind of house? How big? What will be your budget?

- **Medical resources**—will you need close proximity to hospitals or clinics?

- **Romantic relationship**—will you be moving in together, or getting engaged or married?

Some people actually feel increased confidence knowing they have numerous options and can be in control of many variables. Some are expectant and hopeful about what new opportunities happen with a move. Others, however, have the lingering fear of change and of the new challenges ahead.

During Phase 2, *I've Decided to Move*, you can expect to shift more focus onto your relationships. You may feel conflicted about your existing relationships because you will be leaving behind many people you love and cherish.

When you inform your relationships of your decision to move, they might have reactions ranging from happy to sad. Your friends and relatives who expressed grief in Phase 1 may continue to try to get you to change your mind. Others who have let go of trying to hold you back will often help you through the next two phases.

Strategies as You Decide to Move

To lessen feelings of limbo, make a list of what is already decided and what is still uncertain. As more decisions are made, scratch them off the list and add them to a "Decisions We've Made" list. The limbo feeling will then decrease.

- What is already decided or certain?

_____

_____

_____

_____

_____

- What is still undecided or uncertain?

_____

_____

_____

_____

_____

Review your reasons for moving. Choose your top three reasons for moving and the positive implications of these top reasons.

Reason 1:

_____

_____

_____

_____

_____

_____

Reason 2:

_____

_____

_____

_____

_____

_____

Reason 3:

_____

_____

_____

_____

_____

_____

Continue your research to check out all realities of this decision. Keep in mind that you always have a choice and can change your mind.

Phase 3—Plan the Move

What to Expect

By Phase 3, there is little chance of turning back. The decision is final. People face the fact that the move is imminent and they'd better make a plan.

It is now time to focus on the logistics of moving. Some of the typical parts of Phase 3 may include:

- Intensifying the job search and scheduling interviews to learn more about the business or organization they are applying to and meeting new people.

- Laying plans for housing in the new location.

- Notifying the landlord or putting your home on the market.

People might feel like their feet are in both locations. They may feel excitement about a new job, business, home, activities, and friends in the new location. However, they may also feel sadness or grief (even if this is a happy move) about leaving certain people, their home, or their job.

In Phase 3 you will make plans for how you will keep in touch with those they leave behind. The family and friends who don't want you to move will have to accept this fact. You will have to be emphatic about this change in their lives and lay plans for maintaining these relationships but from a distance. The plan will also focus on how to start establishing new relationships in the new location.

Strategies as You Plan the Move

- Don't wait to plan for the upcoming move.

- Since moving is stressful and fatiguing, plan how you will take care of yourself. This is the time to review the suggestions for coping with stress found at the end of this chapter. Plan carefully so you get sufficient sleep, you exercise, and eat right.

- Read one of the books on moving listed in the appendix that cover the logistics of moving such as changing address, notifying utilities, selecting movers, etc. Follow the checklists found in these books.

- Determine what you are taking and what items you will be leaving behind. Clean out the old and useless stuff. Hold a garage sale and/or give items to your favorite charity's thrift shop. Select items for the gifts you can give to your Keepers and colleagues.

- Get extra help with sorting, selling, giving away, and then packing your possessions.

- Lay the groundwork for the transition to the new job in the new location or complete your plans for ensuring a successful transition for your own business.

- Plan farewell events and rituals.

- If you plan an advance trip to tie up loose ends in the new location, use this opportunity to start meeting new people. Your first relationships might be the people you meet while finalizing your housing situation, taking out insurance, and perhaps visiting the school your children will attend. These people might offer new referrals to doctors, dentists, lawyers, vets, or other contacts and service people you will need once moved.

Phase 4—Make the Move

What to Expect

Phase 4 is the final phase. This involves the physical act of moving, settling in, and seriously seeking new relationships. During this phase, people often think, "I'm so ready to move out and to move in!" or "Let the adventures begin!" or "We've survived so far and we know we will thrive in our new home".

Others may still be unhappy, anxious, and stressed until they accept their decision to move. Most feel overwhelmed with settling in, starting a new job, and meeting new people because everything is new and happening all at once. Fatigue is common in this final phase because of the expenditure of energy and time to get settled.

If you are beginning a new job, it usually takes several months to become thoroughly oriented with the organization and job responsibilities.

If you are starting up a business in this new location, it will require hard work and patience. There is endless unpacking, perhaps redecorating, and shopping for items you need.

In this phase, those people you left behind will be wondering and even worrying about how you are. Your cherished family and friends will want to hear from you. Moving on means making a concerted effort to establish new relationships. You may wonder if you are ready and able to *Say Hello* to new relationships.

Strategies for Making the Move

- Follow the checklists of tasks for moving. You can check them off as they are accomplished.

- Relish your personal items as you unpack and find just the right place for them in your new home.

- Put photos of your Keepers, your family, and your friends, in a prominent spot.

- Implement your plan for staying in touch with your Keepers and other people important to you. Your first task is to let them know you have arrived at your new location and let them know how you are doing.

- You will find ideas in Chapter 7 for seeking and cementing new relationships. For example, on your calendar mark down events you will attend in your first month. Take time to explore the new area more. You are sure to meet more people that way too.

Expect to Be Stressed

Every move we make will have some degree of stress. Expect to be stressed during all four phases of moving. In Peter Hanson's book, *Stress for Success,* there is a list of life events that cause stress with death of a spouse, financial distress, and divorce getting the highest rankings. Moving is right up at the top in ranking as well, since a move involves several events: an unstable home and personal life, instability in relationships, travel, and changes in jobs, residence, and schools.

How you deal with your stress will affect the outcome of your transformation; the choice will be yours!

Ironically, one person may claim that moving is a less than favorable situation while the same situation might be seen as a very favorable situation for another. Rate yourself on how stressed you get when you move (either your last move or the upcoming one) by circling one of the numbers on the scale below.

1	2	3	4	5
Totally Relaxed		**Moderately Stressed**		**Totally Stressed**

You can decide to make the best of lemons by making lemonade with a realistic but positive plan. Use the following suggestions for dealing with stress while you go through the four phases of moving.

- **Name your stressors.** Every time you feel stressed during this moving transition, write down what is happening to cause this particular stress. Does this remind you of past moves that were unpleasant? How?

_____

_____

_____

_____

_____

- **Do whatever you need to do to calm down:** taking deep breaths, repeating an affirmation like, "I can handle this problem", or taking a walk.

- **Be positive.** People who assume a positive attitude and pro-actively deal with the causes of their stress will keep stress levels in check.

- **Seek help** with your stress by reading books or talking with friends.

- **Seek professional help** for intense stress to regain your sense of control over your life.

- **Exercise often.** You will be calmer because exercise takes your mind off your to-do list of moving tasks. Exercise can also help you concentrate better on all of those tasks.

- **Eat right!** During this moving transition, you especially need to avoid fast food that is full of carbohydrates and sugar. Instead, eat lots of fruits and vegetables for your carbs and low-fat meat and fish for protein. Your body might not crave the sugar, but your mind might.

- **Cry.** Tears actually provide a bodily reaction because they carry away negative stress chemicals such as manganese and prolactin.

- **Say "No" to everything** you can so you can focus on the important tasks.

- **Prioritize your tasks** and stay focused only on one task at a time.

Chapter 4

What's Your Moving Style?

Four Moving Styles

What style do you use when you make major decisions in your life, especially about a move?

Dr. Carl Jung researched, developed, and tested his theories about how people consistently react in certain situations. He created descriptions for four behavioral styles. This model has been used in both therapeutic and personal development settings. In this book, Jung's proven model is used to describe the four different ways people approach a move and how they deal with the resulting changes in their relationships.

Style A, **Intuitor**, is someone who...

- Abstractly grasps potential problems and possible solutions related to the upcoming move.

- Primarily trusts their gut reaction when meeting new people.

- Uses their intuitive reaction to make decisions and move forward even when information is limited or unavailable.

Style B, **Sensor**, is someone who...

- Quickly accepts the reasons for and reality of the upcoming move.

- Immediately identifies and acts on the bottom line of the upcoming move.

- Acts quickly to resolve interim challenges during the moving transition.

Style C, **Thinker**, is someone who…

- Uses a conceptual, logical, analytical approach to the move.

- Researches and analyzes relevant information about people, places and things before acting.

- Acts in an organized manner based on prior analysis of collected data.

Style D, **Feeler**, is someone who…

- Focuses on how emotions and relationships are affected by the upcoming move.

- Recognizes and expresses their own feelings about the move.

- Empathizes with others' feelings regarding the move.

To determine your dominant style, think about a previous move and answer the questions for each style. Place a checkmark next to each one you generally used.

Intuitor

Are you someone who…

- ☐ Abstractly grasps potential problems and possible solutions related to the upcoming move?

- ☐ Primarily trusts your gut reaction when meeting new people?

- ☐ Uses your intuitive reaction to make decisions and move forward, even when information is limited or unavailable?

Sensor

Are you someone who...

- ❏ Quickly accepts the reasons for and reality of the upcoming move?

- ❏ Immediately identifies and acts on the bottom line of the upcoming move?

- ❏ Acts quickly to resolve interim challenges during the moving process?

Thinker

Are you someone who...

- ❏ Uses a conceptual, logical, and analytical approach to the move?

- ❏ Researches and analyzes relevant information about people, places, and things before acting?

- ❏ Acts in an organized manner based on prior analysis of collected data?

Feeler

Are you someone who...

- ❏ Focuses on how emotions and relationships are affected by the upcoming move?

- ❏ Recognizes and expresses their own feelings regarding the move?

- ❏ Empathizes with others' feelings about the move?

Record the number of responses you checked under each style.

Intuitor _____

Sensor _____

Thinker _____

Feeler _____

The style you checked the most is your #1 style or primary way you approach moving. Your #2 style is your secondary or backup style that you use less often. If two styles have the same top number, this means that you use both styles, often shifting your behavior to best fit the situation.

Follow Four People on Their Journeys

To help you understand each style better, read about the following people:

- Margaret, the Intuitor
- Laura and Leslie, both Sensors
- Bob, the Thinker
- Sally, the Feeler

Read each person's story, noting their primary and secondary styles, moving history, attitude towards moving, the reasons for their last move, and what they thought, felt, and did during each of the four phases of their Moving Model.

As your read their stories, pay attention to when something these people think, feel, act upon is similar to your own approach to moving. This will help you to confirm your primary and secondary styles or approaches to moving.

Margaret, the Intuitor

Margaret's primary behavioral style is **Intuitor.** She knew her reasons for moving, resolved each challenge, and informed her family and current friends of her decision to move.

Margaret moved about five times since she left home. She had a youthful adventure in Europe. She furthered her education at several colleges. When she turned 30, she moved to Oregon and lived there for 25 years.

Phase 1: Margaret intuits about moving.

For years, Margaret knew that someday she'd make a change in location to create a new chapter in her life. She lived in the Northwest since college. For a long time, she was drawn to the state of Colorado.

At midlife, a difficult divorce plus her son's upcoming high school graduation gave her the motivation to do something different. With a certificate as a Life Coach and experience in helping her clients solve problems, she had confidence she could successfully face and solve problems with moving and building new relationships.

Margaret said, "I knew this move would have an impact on my current relationships. As I thought about missing my closest relationships, I also knew I needed this change."

Phase 2: Margaret decides to move and takes a closer look at her relationships.

As her son's high school graduation got closer and he was accepted at the University of Colorado, she decided to take the leap. Once she made the decision, she became excited and optimistic, qualities often found in an Intuitor.

She addressed any lingering concerns, like uncertainty about jobs and locations in Colorado, but allayed these fears by gathering some information.

She trusted her ability to figure out how to deal with leaving behind many long-term friends and colleagues and finding new ones to fill her life. She knew she needed to approach her friends carefully about her decision. Margaret openly shared her decision. She wasn't surprised that some of her colleagues and friends were sad or apprehensive about her decision and tried to dissuade her.

Others asked questions, but did not try to talk her out of moving. They wished the best for her. Margaret wisely chose a few of her well-wishers to freely share all of her thoughts and feelings. They helped her think through additional options and potential problems. This helped her confirm what her intuition was telling her.

Phase 3: Margaret lays plans to move and how to "Say Goodbye".

Margaret knew she was not turning back. No longer was she in limbo about her decision. She was ready to move forward.

Job prospects prompted an advance trip to Colorado. This helped her trim her list of possible locations. She decided to try a totally new behavior. She felt the need to take time finding both a job and housing. As a temporary measure, she decided to be a house-sitter. She was increasingly excited about this new chapter in her life.

Typical of an Intuitor, she did not make a detailed plan on how she would stay in touch with her favorite people. She intuitively knew it would happen. Margaret said, "I already held them in my heart so I had every intention to keep in touch with them."

But saying good-bye was not easy. As the moving date got closer, both grief and many happy memories bubbled up.

There were farewell events and parties. She gave gifts or expressed her affection in poems and letters. Her son's graduation was a rite of passage celebration. As a longtime swimmer, she swam one last time in the ocean as she thanked and praised the waters that gave her so much joy.

Phase 4: Margaret moves and accelerates her immersion into Colorado.

A friend drove with Margaret to her new home state. Margaret recalled, "When we reached the last high point of the drive over the Rocky Mountains and could see Denver laid out below, my fears, grief, and doubts suddenly hit me! 'What am I doing? Maybe I should turn around'." She acknowledged the feelings but quickly shifted her attention because she just knew she'd survive.

Margaret, at her own pace, stayed in touch with her key friends back in Oregon. She called them often and emailed stories about her new adventures. She flew back three times in the first year.

Margaret built upon the earlier groundwork for this re-launching process. As she met new people, she listened to her inner self to assess if they would be appropriate friends.

She knew which groups, associations, clubs, and recreational activities had benefited her before. She attended workshops, talks, and even a conference. She had no outdoor place to swim, but she decided to hike and bike instead.

Laura and Leslie, the Sensors

Laura and Leslie's primary style as Sensors meant that they grasped situations quickly and analyzed and drew conclusions easily. Once a decision was made, they put the past behind them and moved forward.

Laura and Leslie were widowed for several years. They met at a dance class. Both realized that they were ready for a change in their lives. Following a short courtship, they married and decided to retire.

Phase 1: Laura and Leslie sensed about moving.

Once Laura and Leslie knew they were committed to one another, they began to talk about their new life together. They compared what they both loved and disliked about the various homes and locations they had lived in. They reached agreement that they preferred

- a warmer climate
- a smaller home with less maintenance
- a moderately-sized city with a dance club
- access to excellent health care
- a body of water good for fishing

Phase 2: Laura and Leslie decide to move.

Laura and Leslie wasted no time in making the decision to move. They decided to make a major move to a totally different climate because they were tired of the winters in upstate New York. They accepted that there would be many challenges ahead, including leaving many good friends and finding a new home.

They research two regions of the United States: the southeast and the southwest. They knew some people living in both regions. With their criteria in mind, they reviewed the southwestern states of Arizona and New Mexico and the southeastern states of Florida and Georgia. The winning state was Florida.

After making this decision, they sent an email announcing their upcoming move to everyone—family, friends, colleagues, neighbors, and people who provided various services such as plumbers, mechanics, etc. They used their contact database to continuously update people as their plans gelled.

Since they were simultaneously going through three transitions at the same time—retirement, new marriage, and a move—they talked often with family and close friends about their thoughts, feelings, and options for handling their mixed emotions.

**Phase 3: Laura and Leslie plan the move
and "Say Goodbye."**

Once the decision was made to move to Florida, they never looked back! The two love birds made their checklists for moving to a new love nest.

With their houses on the market and some promising activity, they took a trip to their new hometown of Daytona Beach to scout out homes. They used the trip to also to meet people referred to them.

Using the Internet, they continued their research on people, organizations, clubs, faith communities, recreational activities, and health resources. They learned the important information about their favorite faith communities and organizations.

They admitted to one another that sometimes they felt grief over leaving some of their dearest relationships. One evening they sat down and developed a plan for how they'd stay in touch with their favorite people. This plan included buying a RV to take a trip back north in the summer. With the plan thought out, Laura and Leslie were prepared to tell others how they would stay in touch.

There were several good-bye events where they shared their appreciation for their friendships and explained how they would stay in touch. They also recommended, in a true Sensor fashion, that, "If you decide to move too, once you make the decision, don't look back. Stay in the present and expect adventures to come your way."

Their closest friends threw a surprise party for them with gag gifts, funny stories about happy times, and toasting—all captured on video. Neighbors arranged to have them come for dinner the three nights before the move because they knew how tired they'd be and wouldn't want to cook.

Phase 4: Laura and Leslie move and accelerate their immersion.

Laura and Leslie drove from New York to Florida. As they crossed the border into Florida, they looked at one another and said, "We're home!"

As Laura and Leslie were unpacking, they left time every day to walk and drive around their new hometown. Using information from their research, they immediately visited some faith communities, favorite clubs, and a dance at the Senior Center.

Their weekly goal was to meet 1 to 2 new people. They assessed their qualities and interests and how they fit in with their own. They followed up with the best prospects, often inviting them to their home for a meal. By the end of their first month, Laura and Leslie were already feeling settled in.

They advised that, "Building friendships takes time. Be open to all the different types of people you meet."

Bob, the Thinker

As a Thinker, Bob spends most of his time researching, systematically recording what he finds, and carefully analyzing his options before acting. He prefers facts and data to people.

Bob grew up in a military family. As an Army brat, he attended eight different schools from the age of 5 to 18. After graduating from college, Bob interviewed members of different military branches and eventually decided to join the Army. He was recommended for Officer's Training School. He moved several times: to Germany, Washington State, Korea, and finally back stateside. Bob thrived in this orderly lifestyle.

Phase 1: Bob thinks about moving.

During his 20 years in the army, Bob knew first-hand how frequent moves impacted military families. He did not want to marry and raise a family under those conditions. However, he bonded with many of his fellow soldiers and their families. With plenty of time to consider his next career move, Bob weighed over and over the merits of continuing in the Army or retiring after 20 years of active duty.

One of the benefits of military life is security. It provides its people with jobs, housing, food, and an automatic community of like-minded people. Bob was so used to this security that he could not entertain the idea of retiring from the Army until he had a job in the outside world.

Bob was stationed at Fort Lewis near Seattle, Washington, and liked the climate, recreational opportunities, and the ocean. Over time, he used his leave to travel to other places in the state. As a Thinker, he did research about additional locations, especially along the coast.

Phase 2: Bob decides to move.

Bob no longer wanted to remain single. He was ready to marry and have a family. This goal tipped the scales to motivate him to find a new job and to move to that location.

He told his Commander about his decision and filed the proper papers for his retirement. Based on his experience as a logistics expert in the Army, he thought his skills would be marketable in many companies. He decided to settle in Seattle because he knew there were a large number of companies there.

He told very few people of his decision because relationships took second seat to finding a new job.

Phase 3: Bob plans his move.

Bob very carefully researched and analyzed jobs in supply chain. His search went smoothly. He had interviews with a variety of companies and landed a very good offer that met his criteria.

Now that his employment was secured, he turned his attention to housing. All of his housing experiences were from living at college and in the military. He tackled the unknown world of real estate when he decided it was time to buy his first house. A knowledgeable realtor helped him with this house hunt. As a Thinker, he had to see many, many houses before making the final decision on one.

He finally told his military buddies and others about his plans to leave the Army. Of course, they were pleased he would be only an hour away.

Phase 4: Bob moves.

Now Bob could move forward with his new life as a civilian. As a typical Thinker, his well-thought-out plan included a checklist of all the logistical tasks of moving. Bob's Army buddies helped him move his furniture and other stuff to his new house. He fed his friends pizza and beer after the truck was unloaded.

He missed some of his best military friends, so he went back for some visits. Once he got his big screen television set, he invited some of them to his house for Super Bowl Sunday.

The house seemed so quiet after years of living on military bases. After a while, he realized he needed to proactively fill a need for some new relationships. He found the people at work friendly and adventuresome. Bob gradually met neighbors as he watered his lawn and took his new dog for walks.

He volunteered at the Humane Society. While there one Saturday, he met a woman who sparked his interest. They say that opposites attract; she was an Intuitor and Feeler, both qualities that would add balance to Bob's Thinking style. The two took their dogs on lots of walks and hikes. Having been a bachelor for so long and with a Thinker style, it took Bob quite a while to get used to the idea of getting married. He eventually married her.

Bob's advice was, "Use your thinking cap to make decisions, but as I've learned from my wife, tap into your feelings and intuition too. It is hard to try on other styles, but with encouragement and practice, it is possible. I did!"

Sally, the Feeler

As a Feeler, Sally is someone who is comfortable with her own feelings and expresses them freely. She easily recognizes others' feelings. She prefers people over information.

Sally grew up in the Omaha area and lived in the same house until she left for college. Her parents, two siblings, and several aunts and uncles lived in the area. She and her husband, Jim, graduated from the University of Nebraska. Together, they had many friends from growing up and going through high school and college together.

Their wedding was held one month after graduation. They lived in an apartment in the city that was near both of their jobs. When Sally had her first child, she quit her job to raise their daughter.

Her relationships were her world. She embraced her family members and friends from her heart. Every Sunday, they had dinner with either her parents or her husband's parents. Holidays were full of social events.

Phase 1: Sally thinks and feels about moving.

Sally was pregnant with their second child. The apartment was already bulging with baby furniture and toys.

Jim was on the fast track with his company and was offered a promotion, but on the opposite end of the metropolitan area in which they lived. Sally expressed her concerns about the increased traffic to work making a longer commute time for Jim and its impact on their family. In Jim's new management position, they realized they would soon need to entertain more frequently with his colleagues and clients. Their daughter was almost ready for Kindergarten, so they felt it might be an appropriate time to move into a community with a solid school system.

Sally often worried that a move would negatively affect their many relationships. She was scared of the pending void in her life. She dreaded the increased time necessary to visit her friends and family.

Some days she felt excited about finding a house that she could decorate. Other days she worried they wouldn't find a home they could afford. When Jim came home, she usually had some new feeling to tell him about. He listened and accepted whatever she felt. In turn, Sally listened closely to his concerns and suggestions for their first home.

Phase 2: Sally and Jim decide to move.

Sally and Jim took their time to make the big decision. During a night out to celebrate their anniversary, they toasted one another and their wonderful marriage. They reviewed their thoughts about moving. They decided to move before the baby's birth. Their apartment days were now behind them.

Sally immediately let everyone know about their decision and reassured them that they wouldn't be moving too far away. Sally felt relieved that most of her friends and family accepted their decision.

They decided they would buy a large enough home for their expanding family, for entertaining, and for overnight guests. A large kitchen that opened to a family room plus a large backyard were also on their wish list for their new home.

Phase 3: Sally and Jim plan the move.

With only six months before the baby was due, they divided up the tasks of planning for the move. Jim used the Internet to research school districts and suggested three. With a large metro map, they highlighted these areas to search for their home.

While her daughter was in pre-school, Sally used their wish list to look at the three suburban communities with the good schools. Her realtor showed her houses that were for sale within these communities. Sally exuded enthusiasm as she told Jim, both their parents, and her best friends about the house hunting trips. She increasingly felt confident that they would find their dream house. Jim joined her on nights and weekends to help evaluate the houses on their short list. Since Sally valued others' opinions, they invited some friends and family to view their top three choices. Sally and Jim quickly put their first choice for a house under contract.

Sally had nurtured so many friendships and helped many friends move. Now, she had plenty of help sorting, packing, picking paint colors, and moving in. They laughed with one another and freely expressed other feelings, too.

Some friends expressed fears that the longer drive between each other would mean they would not see Sally very often. She always listened and then emphatically reassured them of her intention to maintain a close relationship.

Phase 4: Sally moves and makes more friends.

On moving day, Sally felt some sadness because she knew it would be somewhat difficult to separate herself from the people she loved. When the old and new furniture was in place, the boxes were unpacked, and the barbeque was set up, they had a huge Open House! With so many extra hands to help with the food and their favorite people's "oohs" and "ahhs", Sally felt that the house was now their home.

With two months left before the new baby's arrival, Sally took on the task to help their daughter adjust because she was sad about leaving her pre-school friends. Sally took her on new adventures. They met the neighborhood children, enjoyed the local park and zoo, and visited her new school.

Sally used referrals from their neighbors and new friends to select doctors and a dentist. She located the home improvement and hobby stores, visited local family restaurants, and established accounts at a local bank. Now she felt secure knowing their family had what they needed.

Sally was able to relax the last month before their son was born. She reflected on how happy and satisfied she felt.

Her advice for other Feelers would be: "Once you are in your new location, be open to explore the area and embrace new people. Moving can be scary, but incredibly exciting as well! Stay in touch regularly with your best friends and family members. Invite them to visit you."

How will your style help you through your move?

At the beginning of this chapter, you learned about Jung's four behavioral styles and identified your own dominant style. Then you learned how four people, each with a dominant style, approached moving and handled their relationships.

Review your assessment on pages 38 and 39 and keep it in mind as you list or describe how you are likely to approach your next move.

List or describe how you will approach your next move.

_____

_____

_____

_____

_____

_____

_____

_____

_____

Your personality style(s) are second nature to you and will help you through a move. Since you are comfortable with them, use them through the four phases of the moving process.

However, if you are struggling, perhaps you need to try something else. Review the other styles and try one you don't usually use. For example, if you are a Sensor and having difficulty, try the behaviors of a Thinker. This next move is your opportunity to transform your life in some positive ways, so give other styles a chance to show their worth.

Don't Do This Without Help!

Are you someone who is reluctant to ask others for help? People who don't ask for help do so for a variety of reasons:

- They like to be independent of other people
- They think they can handle a situation
- It just might be their style to go it alone

Which style will ask for help? Each style type can ask for help, but will do so in their own way:

- The Intuitor will know just who can and will help.
- The Sensor will contact helpful friends without delay, sensing the clock is ticking toward deadlines.
- The Thinker will initially think they can manage, but later will realize that extra hands would be beneficial and a logical thing to do.
- The Feeler will be grateful to people who offer to help and will let them know how that makes them feel.

Are you ready to ask for help?

Join the Crowd!

The previous three chapters covered your moving history, the Four Phases of the Moving Model, and clarifications of your own personality style. Let's move on to exploring your current relationships, selecting the best ones to keep and discarding some others. Join the millions of people who move, but this time with a new perspective about how your relationships are impacted.

Chapter 5

Retain the Best!

An Unusual Benefit

With my knowledge of moving, I've discovered one clear benefit that I would like to share. Before the moving truck was loaded, we cleaned out the old and useless stuff and kept only our treasures. The task of sorting all of the gear we accumulated was time consuming but had many benefits. During the process, we recognized that we were not only thinking about things but about the people around us. Discarding the things that were no longer needed helped to save on moving costs and allowed us the time to pay attention to our relationships. We sorted through our list of friends, colleagues, neighbors, club, and church members and crossed off the names of those whom we believed we would have no future need to be in contact with after each move.

As I watched many other people move, I discovered that most were so busy with the logistics of moving, like packing and changing addresses, that they forgot to invest some energy into their current and future relationships.

How sad it would be that as you are unpacking your books, you suddenly remembered that you forgot to contact your previous book club members. One of the reasons I wrote this book is so that your most important relationships won't be forgotten. I also believe that your next move will give you the opportunity to change your personal and professional relationships for the better by focusing on those most important to you.

In this chapter, you will identify your most treasured people, called *Keepers*, who you will retain after you move. You will sort out those who you have no further reason to stay in contact with after you move and Drop contact with them. You will also identify and initially keep some contact with people called *Occasionals*.

Who Comes to Dinner Now?

Years ago, I learned a valuable clarification process that explored one's core values. I encourage you to think about this and apply your values in all aspects of your life. This process truly enriched my personal and professional life. I clarified my values and consciously chose better relationships.

One particular activity from that training was most helpful. The premise was that when we eat and drink with others, we bond at a deeper level. Think about this...would you choose to go to lunch with someone at work who grates on your nerves? Of course not! When you want to have fun, do you invite people you find boring to join you? Definitely not!

Three Kinds of Relationships

Keepers are people you love and appreciate, or those people with whom you have a strong need to stay in touch. These special people add value to your life, support you in challenging times, spend some holidays with you, remember your birthday, and call, text, or email you regularly. These people are real gems, your Keepers. You want to keep contact with them after you move.

I met Cheryl 20 years ago when I reviewed her project for certification in our profession. I instinctively knew she was a person I'd want to get to know more deeply. She was conscientious and willing to accept feedback. She was excited about leaving a job in dentistry to become a facilitator/trainer.

Before long, we met for dinner and found we had many common personal interests. Since she was about to move closer to her fiancé, I helped her think through various job opportunities. Once she was working in the Denver area, she would invite me to lunch to meet some of her interesting colleagues.

We were honored to be a part of her wedding celebration. We also enjoyed celebrating the birth of their daughter who, to this day, calls me "Aunty Lois." We get together often, sharing life's challenges, strategizing work goals, and always celebrating birthdays together. Cheryl is one of my closest Keepers.

Occasionals are those you have enjoyed as acquaintances or colleagues, or whose presence in your life has occasionally been beneficial to you and to them. They stay in touch less often. For whatever reason, you don't want to drop them completely from your radar, so you put them in the Occasional contact category.

I met Nancy 25 years ago at a women's association. She was a friendly and enthusiastic person. Along with our husbands, we began getting together to go to plays and would occasionally invite each other to dinner.

As their children started school and became teens, I noticed a change. We rarely heard from them but when we did, our conversations were still lively. Over the years, especially since we had moved further away, we got together less and less. They became Occasional friends.

People to **Drop** are those who are hard to be around or have outgrown their usefulness. You may have benefited from knowing them at some time, but your needs or theirs have changed. These people can be left behind and you will see that it is best to discontinue contact with them.

My relationship with Marilyn started out fine. Since she was an experienced trainer, I invited her to join me in a new leadership development project. I welcomed her ideas and experience. Later, her true colors emerged. Nothing was good enough; she criticized a lot and gave unsolicited and negative feedback. She needed to be the star. She would blurt out whatever she was thinking, whether it was helpful or not. She never understood how her behaviors affected others. Marilyn was a person I Dropped.

Make Your Lists

The table below shows the names of my relationships in the three categories.

CURRENT WORK RELATIONSHIPS				
Name	**No. Years Known**	**Keeper**	**Occasional**	**Drop**
Harry	15		O	
Charlotte	8	K		
Linda	4			D
Marilyn	2			D
Jerry	6		O	

CURRENT COMMUNITY AND NEIGHBORHOOD RELATIONSHIPS				
Name	**No. Years Known**	**Keeper**	**Occasional**	**Drop**
Anne and Bill	8		O	
Veronica	2			D
Vickie & Tim	5			D
Marylou	10	K		

CURRENT FRIENDS				
Name	**No. Years Known**	**Keeper**	**Occasional**	**Drop**
Cheryl	20	K		
Kaye and J	15		O	
Joan	6	K		
Betsy	11		O	
Dave	3		O	
Becky & Patrick	5			D
Lila	2			D

Retain the Best!

List the names of your work and community connections and neighbors and friends who currently are involved in your life. Next to each name, write down how many years you have had a relationship with them or when you first met them.

CURRENT WORK RELATIONSHIPS				
Name	No. Years Known	Keeper	Occasional	Drop

CURRENT COMMUNITY AND NEIGHBORHOOD RELATIONSHIPS				
Name	No. Years Known	Keeper	Occasional	Drop

CURRENT FRIENDS				
Name	**No. Years Known**	**Keeper**	**Occasional**	**Drop**

Code Every Relationship

Think about the people on your lists and decide what characteristics and criteria are most important to you.

Code each person with a K for Keeper, O for Occasional, or D for Drop.

- Put K next to each person who is a Keeper and with whom you will sustain a meaningful relationship even at a long distance.

- Put O next to each person with whom you enjoy a relationship, but not as meaningful a relationship as your Keepers. The Occasional designation might be more difficult to assign, leaving you conflicted, unsure, and feeling guilty. Some people might have started out as Keepers but the relationships have shifted as time has moved on.

- Put D next to each person who you'll Drop and make no contact with them when you move. You may feel sad, angry, relieved, or maybe surprised. It is time to drop those relationships that are no longer mutually beneficial or were never close to begin with.

Review the Drop List First

By now you should be clear about the characteristics you value and benefit from in your relationships, both personal and professional. Start with your Drop list. Scan the names of the people you coded with a **D**. Answer the following questions:

1. What is it about these D people that you can walk away from them and have no further contact?

   _____

   _____

   _____

   _____

   _____

   _____

   _____

2. What characteristics do these D people possess? For example:
   - Stopped responding to your texts, emails, and calls?
   - A lack of loyalty?
   - Outgrown my interests and values?
   - Untrustworthy?
   - Won't be living by nor working together anymore?
   - Other: _____

Let's drop them now!

You know who you can Drop and why. The people you will drop most likely don't possess those characteristics you cherish and deserve or need the most, or you were never really close with that person to begin with.

Go through your database and eliminate them! Get rid of this clutter.

1. How does that feel?

_____

_____

_____

_____

_____

_____

2. What have you learned from this exercise?

_____

_____

_____

_____

_____

_____

Learn from this clarification process.

When you meet new people in your new hometown, avoid relationships similar to those you just dropped. Change your approach and be wary. Don't repeat the same mistakes.

There are important benefits for dropping people from your life. You will have more time for your Keepers, for making new and better friends, for deepening relationships with only the best colleagues. You will have more time to enjoy your new location.

I'll Contact You...Occasionally

Next, review your list of Occasional relationships to decide why you want to stay in contact with them, although only occasionally.

Review the names of the people you coded with an **O.** Answer the following questions:

1. What is it about the O people that you want to keep some future contact with them?

_____

_____

_____

_____

_____

_____

2. What characteristics, attitudes, or skills do these people possess that once enhanced your life? For example:

- We share a common interest or hobby
- We've been in a relationship a long time
- I enjoyed working with them once.
- I don't want to burn any bridges with some professional contacts.

_____

_____

_____

_____

_____

_____

Instead of Dropping them completely from your contacts, create an Occasional group.

- Contacts will be made less frequently. For example, you might contact them once a month, then quarterly. At the end of your first year in the new location, you might only contact them with a Holiday card or e-newsletter.

- Email messages will get shorter, although still newsy.

- You might call some occasionally.

Retain the Best as Your Keepers

Finally, review your Keepers list and why you will keep them in your life after you move.

Review the names of the people you coded with a **K.** Answer the following question:

1. What characteristics, attitudes or skills do these Keepers possess that consistently enhance my life? For example:

   - She stuck by me during good and bad times.
   - He went out of his way to help me sort job offers.
   - She always answered my emails, text messages, and phone calls quickly.

You will need to be creative and diligent to maintain contact, especially if they live far away. Let your Keepers know how you plan to stay in touch. Here are some ways to stay in regular contact with your Keepers:

- Use or learn how to use social media sites like Twitter and Facebook for life updates.

- Create a group list of all your Keepers in your contact book.

- Use Twitter and text messaging for shorter messages.

- Email longer messages with more details and send them frequently.

- Call, Skype, or video chat on a regular basis.
- Send photos of your new home and interesting places you frequent.
- Plan periodic trips back to see your Keepers. Invite them to come and see you.
- Plan a vacation together.
- Modify your contact plan as needed. For instance, if you realize that someone relates better with phone calls rather than email, plan a time to call them.

How Many Membership Cards Do You Carry?

You have completed your review of your individual relationships, so let's turn to the groups, clubs, and associations to which you belong. Depending on your needs and available time, they can play a very important role in your new life.

This activity starts with filling in the chart below with specific names of all the organizations you are involved in where you *currently* live. Put the names under the column "Current Memberships".

Current Groups, Clubs, and Associations

Code	Organizations	Current Memberships	Might Join in New Location	Actually Joined within 2 Years after a Move
	Associations			
	Faith Community			
	Clubs			

Current Groups, Clubs, and Associations (concluded)

Code	Organizations	Current Memberships	Might Join in New Location	Actually Joined within 2 Years after a Move
	Learning Opportunities			
	Networking or Support Group			
	Political Groups			
	Recreational and Sport Groups or Clubs			

Now assign a code for every organization you've listed above:

VB = Very Beneficial and Satisfactory
SB = Somewhat Beneficial and Satisfactory
RB = Rarely Beneficial and Satisfactory

Answer the following questions about the **Very Beneficial and Satisfactory** groups, clubs, and associations:

1. What was it about those **Very Beneficial and Satisfactory** organizations that enhanced your life?

_____

_____

_____

_____

_____

2. Are there common patterns among those coded VB? If so, what are they?

_____

_____

_____

_____

_____

Answer the following questions about the **Somewhat Beneficial and Satisfactory** ones:

1. What was it about the **Somewhat Beneficial and Satisfactory** organizations that enhanced your life? What were they lacking that made them only Somewhat Beneficial?

_____

_____

_____

_____

_____

2. Are there common patterns among those coded SB?

_____

_____

_____

_____

_____

Answer the following questions about the **Rarely Beneficial and Satisfactory** ones:

1. What was it about the **Rarely Beneficial and Satisfactory** ones that was not so beneficial or satisfactory?

_____

_____

_____

_____

_____

2. Are there common patterns among those coded RB?

_____

_____

_____

_____

_____

Look to Your Future

Based on your evaluation, check all the organizations that you might join in your next location.

When you get to Chapter 7, which reviews how to establish new relationships, you will return to this chart to help you find new friends, colleagues, and organizations in your new location.

Chapter 6

Release and Let Go

To everything there is a season,
A time for every purpose under the sun
A time to be born and a time to die
A time to plant and a time to pluck up that which is planted
A time to kill and a time to heal
A time to weep and a time to laugh
A time to mourn and a time to dance
A time to embrace and a time to refrain from embracing
A time to lose and a time to seek
A time to reap and a time to sow
A time to keep silent and a time to speak
A time to love and a time to hate
A time for war and a time for peace.

Ecclesiastes 3:1–8

...and a time to stay and a time to leave.

Leave the Baggage Behind

When the decision to move is made and there is no turning back, it is time to release the grip of the past. Let go of what is holding you back; it is time to say goodbye. "Emotional baggage" is what we carry with us that should be left behind.

If the move is prompted for positive reasons, it may be easier to let go than if the move occurs because of unfortunate circumstances. But regardless of the motive, people need to try to leave the baggage behind so they can move on.

Sherry's husband was a pilot who commuted by plane every week to his airline's hub in another city. He was very happy with his job. After commuting a year, the couple decided it was more important for the family if he wasn't away five days a week. They moved to his employer's city and Sherry became a "trailing spouse" with one small child and no job outside the home.

For two years, she yearned to be back with her family and dear friends in their previous location. She could fly for free, so she returned frequently. However, she could not let go of the baggage of her past life in her new life.

When people continue to carry their baggage to a new location, they remain weighed down by missing people and yearning for the life they left behind. They cannot fully immerse in the new community, job, or school. They have a foot in both locations and are pulled back and forth. This chapter will help you to *Release and Let Go* so you *can* move on.

People who are more in touch with their emotions, or "Feelers", are generally aware of the variety of emotions when letting go. If you are not a Feeler, you will need to work harder to identify your feelings.

Find a quiet place. Close your eyes for a few minutes and reflect on your reasons for moving and whether or not it is a happy choice, because of difficult circumstances, or job-related. Pay attention to all of the feelings that emerge.

Is This Move Your Choice?

Now look at your move from both perspectives—if the move is your choice and if it isn't your choice. Whether or not this is your choice will affect your willingness to release the past and move on. When you don't perceive this as your choice, you can feel powerless. When you do perceive this as your choice, you'll feel empowered and more invigorated to move forward.

Here is Phil's example of a move that **was not** his choice. Read what he thought about the move and how he felt.

What I'll Leave Behind	What I'll Take With Me
Dear friends	Sadness that I won't see them
A job that I enjoyed	I can apply what I learned to my next job

Feelings That Emerge:
Sadness
Uncertainty about my future
Some depression
Knowing I'm in limbo

Moving? Saying Goodbye and Saying Hello!

Here is Marie's example whose move **was** her choice.

What I'll Leave Behind	What I'll Take With Me
A beautiful house we built	House plans to use again
A core of close friends	I have great memories; I already plan to return often.
Residue of a very bad work conflict and those who contributed to the problem	Peace of mind that I did my best and what this taught me

Feelings That Emerge:

Optimistic

Some sadness

Assurance I can find new friends

Determined to handle conflicts better

Release and Let Go

Now fill in your own chart. Write down what feelings emerge when you think about what you'll leave behind and what you will take with you to a new location.

What I'll Leave Behind	What I'll Take With Me

Feelings That Emerge:

Compare the Two Charts

What do you see when you compare the two different perspectives about moving?

The examples of Phil and Maria illustrate that when a move *is not* our choice, a lot of baggage may be carried to the new location. When a move *is* our choice, a positive perspective will carry us forward with a more constructive outlook.

Remember the old adage that tells us to make lemonade out of lemons? Since every move includes at least a few lemons, if not a whole bushel, the key is what we do with them.

The choice is yours. You can choose to work through the grief, sadness, resentment, anger and any other negative feelings. You can choose to open up to the possibility that this move will bring you new adventures, fresh opportunities, wonderful and additional new friends, renewed happiness and sweet lemonade.

Uncertainty, loss, resentment, sadness, and grief are common. No matter the depth of feelings about leaving, accept that there is no fixed time to overcome feelings that may hold you back.

Unprocessed grief can affect you and those you leave behind. It can keep you from starting your new job search or color your ability to embrace new relationships. Here are some ideas to try:

- Write regularly about your thoughts and feelings about moving. Periodically review what you wrote. See if time has shifted your attitudes towards a more positive perspective.

- This writing exercise slows down the left side or logical side of the brain and taps into the right side of your brain, revealing insights and creative ideas that will be helpful to you in dealing with your negativity. With a pencil or pen in your non-dominant hand, write every feeling and thought you have. Just write even if it is strange and awkward. Do not correct spelling or other mistakes…just write. Reflect on how you feel now.

- Make a collage using pictures and words that express your feelings. Find images that symbolize your strongest feelings. What feelings come up? Just let them out. Visualize them flying away.

- Allot some time to "get it out"—take the time to feel your negative feelings. Do this for a limited time starting with 15 minutes. Every week reduce the time by 5 minutes. Express your deepest feelings: grief, loss, anger. Cry, scream, or pound a pillow. Allot a different time every day when you will focus on the positive aspects of moving starting with 5 minutes. Every week increase the time by 5 minutes. As you identify positive possibilities, you will begin to believe there can be positive outcomes to moving.

- Talk with one of your Keepers. Pick someone who is a good listener and who views your move in a positive light, even though you will be leaving them behind. If you pick a Keeper who identifies closely with your feelings, then you'll just have a pity party. Ask this person to just listen and to ask you clarifying questions and to avoid giving any advice. You could ask your Keeper to take some notes. Just keep talking, give examples, and express any emotions that emerge until you reach a point when you have gotten all the feelings out.

- Talk with someone who has moved when it wasn't their choice. Find out how they managed and what advice they might have for you.

- Talk to a professional; someone who specializes in working with people in transition.

Saying Goodbye

How to Say Goodbye to Your Keepers

You have already identified certain people as your Keepers and probably have every intention to stay in contact with them. Since they are so important to you, early on, when you are thinking about a move, make every effort to tell each of these people about your plans. This will mean a lot to them because you have taken time and made the effort to talk face-to-face.

Prepare carefully how you will break the news. Try something like this:

- Invite them for coffee or lunch.

- Start with reminiscing on how you met, one or two positive events or experiences you've shared, and the qualities you appreciate in them.

- Next, give some background about what has been happening in your life that was the catalyst for thinking about moving.

- Then, announce your plan to move.

- Finally, stop and listen to their reactions. Be prepared that some will immediately grieve, express sadness, or challenge your reasons or plans. Others may immediately say that they are happy if you are happy even though they'd rather you didn't have to move away.

If you have privately worked through your decision and feelings accompanying this decision, then it is now important to give those who express sadness about your move time to catch up and resolve their grief.

Listen to their thoughts and feelings. Avoid making judgments and telling a person how they should be feeling.

They might try to induce guilt in you by saying, "How could you leave us?" or "Don't you know I can't live without you here?" You might need to take a stand and remind them gently why you made a decision that will benefit you.

Jennifer could relate to this: "When we made the decision to move out of state, I invited our dear friend to lunch. I told her how important she has been in our lives for over 10 years. Then I reminded her that my husband was still in remission after his treatment for advanced cancer. I explained that we decided not to wait to implement our dreams because we never know how long we have on this earth.

I told her that we visited our chosen state and explained how my husband's eyes lit up when he saw sailboats on the big lake. I decided he should have one more opportunity to sail.

She was shocked at the news. "Why?" she kept asking. She argued about every reason I gave so I stopped trying and listened. I knew this was a terrible blow to her since we had shared happy times and helped each other through some difficult times.

For the next two months, with every phone call and get-together, she made it very clear she didn't want us to move. I gave her reassurances because she needed to know that we would not lose contact nor forget her.

Be prepared—this process may take a lot of time. Expect to hear others repeat their sadness every time you talk. Listen sincerely to their feelings. You might see a shift in those feelings as time goes on.

Reassure those grieving that they are your Keepers. This word resonates well with those who need reassurance that you won't leave them totally. Reaffirm the value of your relationship with them.

Explain specifically how you plan to stay connected with them. If they need to hear your voice, plan to call regularly or video chat. As time goes on, you might need to "wean" them from expecting so many frequent calls.

Use other ideas outlined in Chapter 5 on staying in touch with your Keepers.

Jennifer's story ends well. Our friend Nancy appreciated hearing our plan to stay in touch with her. I said that for the first year, I'd come back every quarter to see her and other Keepers. I explained that I'd pick times when she would be available to get together with me. I suggested she think about making a trip to visit us within six months of our move. I reminded her of the value of today's technology that will make it easy to stay in touch.

Moving? Saying Goodbye and Saying Hello!

When They Are Happy for You

Even those who are generally happy for you and your decision to move will need to hear your reasons for moving.

- Go over your reasons, especially any that might impact them.

- Review your plan for staying in touch, personalizing the plan to fit each Keeper. Solicit how they will stay in touch with you.

- Ask their advice about one or more aspect of your moving plans.

- Once you have broken the news to these Keepers, during the following weeks or months as your moving plans evolve, keep them informed.

Leave a Gift

As you clean out the old and useless stuff in your home and sort what you plan to take with you when you move, find an item you can leave as a gift for some of those you are leaving behind. It may be something you no longer value, but a treasure to one of your dear friends. If you are a crafter, is there something you can make for each special person? If not, you could go out and buy a small gift. The goal is to choose an item or gift that will remind them of you.

Juanita explained how she did this. "Within four weeks of making our decision to move, I had identified my Keepers and wondered what I could leave of me with them.

"I looked over the items in our home that were in our 'give away' pile and those in the 'what should we do with this?' pile. Some items immediately spoke to me and said,' Give these easels to Jay'. Or 'Joanne would love this print of the Hawaiian goddess Pele in their Hawaiian bedroom.' Or, 'Elena has always admired my sculpture of an Indian woman.'

"As I took walks on lovely fall days, I noticed how many different plants there were and had an inspiration. Why not make some gifts with dried plant materials? I collected armloads and made simple gifts for my Keepers.

"What a joy it was to present a unique gift to each person as I saw them. I told them, 'I'm giving you a gift you can use over and over so you won't forget me!' They replied, 'I'll never forget you and thanks so much'."

Get Together Before You Move

Most people who are about to move are invited either out for a meal or a drink or to a Keeper's home. Be sure to make time to accept every invitation.

Some folks plan a large farewell event. At work, it might be a catered lunch in the office or a gathering after work at a local grill. In your personal circle, someone might hold a potluck dinner and invite whomever you want to attend.

In all cases, whether a one-on-one or a group event, be ready to share your own goodbye. This is a time for you to prepare some stories. Think back on everything you have shared with these people and compile your favorite stories. Weave in what you appreciate about them and how you plan to stay in touch.

Come to My Party

With people so busy these days, it can be difficult to find time to prepare meals or parties for others. But don't be disappointed if you do not get many invitations. If you would rather, plan your own "Au revoir" event, party, or open house.

Joan told me about their "Good Egg Party". They invited their best friends and colleagues. Their home was decorated in an egg theme and many of the dishes were connected to this theme. After everyone arrived, Joan and her husband welcomed them and explained that they think of each of them as a "good egg." Then they gave each person a story and a gift. Joan had decorated eggs and prepared what she would say. She asked each person to choose an egg and once done, Joan delivered her heartfelt remarks. Joan explained that when doing this, it is important to make pin pricks in each end of the egg and blow out the yolk and egg white so your friends can keep their egg indefinitely.

Hold a Ritual

A ritual confers dignity upon the departing person, and also provides comfort and closure to those who remain. There are common elements to good ceremonies that honor the parting. The ritual has a planned agenda, but also room for spontaneity and emotion. Some people gather in a sacred or special space where they stand in a circle. There is sharing of stories and memories. Symbols, props, and memorabilia codify the past. Music is often an element. Sometimes a symbolic metaphor is performed, such as setting butterflies free.

The Ties That Bind

During the first three phases of the transition of moving, no matter how thoroughly and thoughtfully you said goodbye to those you are leaving behind, you will need to continue this process during Phase 4: Making the Move.

As you make your way to your new home, you may find yourself thinking about how a close friend might also enjoy the scenery you are seeing. When you realize you have traveled 300, 500, 1,000 or more miles to your new community, it can hit you hard that from now on you won't be able to drop over to visit or go to lunch with your old friends.

As you unpack boxes, certain items will trigger good memories like when you used your china for a New Year's Eve party that was shared with your closest friends.

These are the binds that will pull at your heartstrings. Whatever you feel is natural and normal. The range of feelings is complex for each of us. Don't deny it. After all, you have made a huge change in your life and no one immediately drops the relationships left behind.

The greatest tugs will revolve around your Keepers. You know who they are. When you miss someone, or groups of people, stop for a few moments and take a deep breath. Quietly reflect on how you feel. Think about what you miss about them. Make a note to call or email them within the day. Then get back to what you were doing— take the time to embrace the person you left behind, but don't dwell.

During the process of unpacking and getting settled into your new home, adjusting to a new job and community, you will be tired and stressed. This could leave you with little energy and time to stay in contact with your Keepers. Here are some suggestions:

- Use the group email list you created of your Keepers and Occasional relationships to broadcast news. The first one is a short email to everyone letting them you have arrived safely and what is happening.

- On a weekly basis, make a short list of people you will call, perhaps a few people who you miss the most.

- When you are feeling sad or lonely, contact someone who will be empathetic and supportive.

- During the following weeks, jot down notes of your feelings, impressions, or events you'd like to write about in future emails. Make a plan as to how often you will send a general email to your Keepers and your Occasionals.

- Over the first few months, save newspaper articles, fliers, take pictures, and put them in an envelope. Decide who will receive one of these special packages. Make copies, write a short note, and mail them off. This effort will send your best Keepers the message that you care for them. The material you send will also give them a glimpse of your new life.

You will get a variety of responses or no responses.

- Initially many of your Keepers will write back.

- Some will not reciprocate with a response. After a while, their Keeper designation switches to Occasional. Those Occasionals who never respond might eventually be dropped.

- With time, your group list will dwindle to loyal Keepers who continue to receive Emails, phone calls, and visits.

To everything there is a reason
To decide to move
To grieve and heal
To say Goodbye
To Say Hello.

Chapter 7

Re-Launch in Your New Location

Start Early to Re-Launch in Your New Location

In Chapter 3, you reviewed the Four-Phase Moving Transition Model and Learned what to expect in each phase:

Phase 1: Think about Moving

Phase 2: Decide to Move

Phase 3: Plan the Move

Phase 4: Make the Move

This chapter focuses on building new relationships. It spans all four phases of your move, beginning when you are just thinking about moving and continuing through the actual move and beyond.

The ideas recommended are presented in the order of the phases. Several suggestions on what to do span over several phases.

Search the Internet, Read Books, and Identify People (Phases 1–4)

Starting in the first phase when you are thinking about moving, and through phase 4 when you've already moved, the Internet, books, and people are all resources that will help you learn about your new location and find organizations and people who match your interests, skills, and needs.

As you find prospects and information about your new location, record the contact information and print out background information. For instance, save stories about someone whom you might want to meet, about a business you need to contact, or about an association or club you might want to join. Highlight those that appeal to you.

Bob successfully used his innate thinking skills to prepare for his move. He thoroughly enjoyed doing research on the Internet. First, he made a list of the important criteria for a new location and ranked them. Using key search words like "best places to live," he viewed the top 10 locations based on his criteria. Next, with a new set of search words, he narrowed the list down to one: Seattle, Washington. His ongoing research focused on the city and the surrounding area.

Start a *Saying Hello* Notebook (Phases 1–4)

Begin this project as soon as you start researching. Select a loose-leaf notebook with a front cover sleeve for a picture of your new location. Use dividers to file information as you discover it, such as:

- Background on various locations
- Spiritual groups
- Recreational groups
- Clubs
- Health and medical options
- Learning opportunities
- People to meet
- Personal services (like dry cleaners, massage therapists, and the like)
- Political and governmental
- Professional associations
- Service organizations
- Workout facilities; gyms

Remember Who is Most Important to You! (Phases 2 & 3)

In Chapter 5, you sorted your relationships into three categories: those people you will retain, called Keepers, those with whom you will have Occasional contact, and those you will Drop.

Review your notes about your Keepers and what qualities they possess. When you eventually meet new people, evaluate each new contact against the list of Keepers' qualities. This will help you to identify those who could be a new colleague or friend who ultimately might reside in the Keeper category.

Review the reasons you previously dropped certain people. Plant these reasons clearly in your memory so you don't inadvertently get involved with new people who are unsuited for you. Avoid people who possess the characteristics or attitudes of those you have just dropped!

Periodically evaluate the information you have for the people in your notebook:

- With whom will you connect?
- Who could be a potential colleague or a good friend?

The notebook will grow over time. If you have a chance to take an advance trip to the new location, take the notebook with you as a reference and as a place to store new information.

Visualize Your New Location (Phases 2 & 3)

Visualizing what has not yet happened increases the chances of it actually happening. Theorists who study our brains tell us that our brains don't know the difference between what is real and what is imagined. Therefore, plant some positive images into your brain through your active visualization.

Take a few quiet moments to visualize. Answer the following five questions. Since the goal of this chapter is to find relationships in your new hometown, be sure to visualize who is with you. Write some details about your visualization:

- What is happening?

  _____

  _____

  _____

  _____

  _____

- When is it happening?

  _____

  _____

  _____

  _____

  _____

- Who is with you?

  _____

  _____

  _____

  _____

  _____

- What do you feel?

  _____

  _____

  _____

  _____

  _____

Flesh out the details you have discovered and keep your notes in your notebook. Return to review the notes as you actually meet new people. Are they at all like you imagined?

Collect Referrals (Phases 2–4)

Once you decide to move, you'll need to start informing people you are leaving behind. As you discuss your relocation plans with those in your network, ask them who they know in your new location. You'll be pleasantly surprised as to how many new contacts you can make this way.

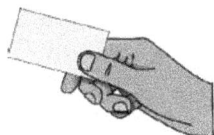

Ask people for details about their referrals, what they are like, their interests and type of work, and how to contact them. Record what you learn. Ask if your friend, relative, or colleague will send an introductory email to them.

Excellent sources for referrals in your new location include realtors, bankers, investment advisors, insurance agent, media professionals, and recruiters. Many professionals in your current location often have a national network and are often happy to share the names of their colleagues in your new location. Remember to file the information you discover in your notebook.

Find Faith Communities, Groups, Clubs, and Associations (Phases 2–4)

Review from Chapter 5 your list of every faith community, group, club, or association you belonged to up to now. Once you have confirmed your decision to move and have made plans for the move, use your list as the starting point for selecting a faith community, groups, clubs, and associations to join in the new location.

If the organization is national, use its membership directory or its website to find out details, including local contacts, activities, and meeting times.

Preparing for an earlier move I made from Michigan to Colorado, I was able to contact the Colorado chapters of three important groups to which I had belonged. I was a member of Zonta (a service club), Toastmasters (a club promoting communication, public speaking, and leadership skills, and the American Society of Training and Development (professional association). Within a few months of moving, I was able to attend my first meeting at each of these three organizations. This suggestion also works when you want to find a new spiritual group.

Since your move can be transformational, consider some new groups, clubs, or associations to explore when you move to a new location. For example, Margaret told me she had always wanted to be a part of a book club, so when she moved, she joined one. Eight years after her move, the people she met through this club are still close friends.

Avoid getting overwhelmed with too many choices by ranking the options. Later, if some don't work out or you want more choices, you can always expand your search using the information you have gathered in your notebook.

Follow the Local News (Phases 2–4)

Subscribe to your new hometown's paper or access news from that city or community through their websites. If you are moving to a new state, subscribe to a state magazine.

For six months before his move, Terry looked forward to receiving the weekly newspaper. First, he'd check the weather to see how it compared to his current location. He'd read the lead stories to gain an understanding of local issues and to learn about the people in local politics and organizations. The community page offered information about local groups, associations, and clubs along with contact information. The service section gave him names of people or business services he would need.

Create a Tag Line (Phase 3)

A "tag line" helps when you begin meeting people face to face. Create a Tag Line that captures who you are, or what you do, or your major interest. Here are some of my examples:

- On our voice mail, we say "Every day is a gift."

- For my business email and card, I quote Susan B. Anthony who said, "Failure is impossible."

> Every day is a gift
>
> Failure is impossible

- For a memory moniker, I say "Hello. My name is Lois Hart. I'm a Matchmaker who connects people with resources."

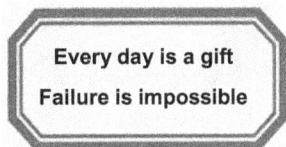

Scout on an Advance Trip (Phase 3)

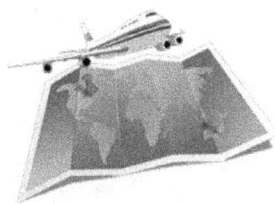

If you take an advance trip to your new location for a job interview or orientation, to choose an apartment or home, or to visit schools, use this opportunity to follow up on some referrals you have been given and also begin to make new contacts. From your notes, select some people and let them know you are coming and want to get together.

At one time, I used the Internet to identify key women in the new location who shared some of my business goals. When visiting the new location, I invited three of these new contacts to lunch.

I stopped in a shop with the intriguing name of "Alpine Tepees." As the owner was sewing on canvas, we chatted. I happened to mention my husband wanted to sail again. He asked about my husband's experience and I asked if he sailed. He offered the use of his sailboat. I had found a very valuable contact!

During your advance visit, take a tour of the city either with a tour company or with one of your new contacts. If you use a realtor, you have the perfect tour guide to help you learn more about the area!

Set Goals and Make a Plan (Phases 3 & 4)

Each of the four personality types have a different approach to setting goals and making plans.

Intuitors don't need a plan and they don't generally worry about whether or not they will find the right people. They may not do much research, but instead they usually wait until they have actually moved. As they meet new people, they just "intuitively know" who is right for them.

Margaret, the **Intuitor:**

- "In three months, I will naturally find some new friends."

- "I will know when I'm ready to reduce the number of trips back home to visit my past relationships."

Feelers tune in easily to other people. This helps them select the "right" people for their lives.

Sally, the **Feeler:**

- "We will have an open house soon after moving in so our friends and family will become familiar with the drive to our new house."

- "We will attend school events and as we meet people, we can decide who 'feels right' for us."

Sensors and Thinkers are most comfortable in relating to many of the ideas in this chapter. Sensors like to jump right in and find new friends and colleagues. Thinkers use their research skills to find new people and groups. Both are organized and save the information they find. Thinkers and Sensors are more likely to set goals for almost everything in their lives.

Laura and Leslie, the **Sensors:**

- "We will visit local faith communities immediately."

- "Every week we will call or visit with one or two new people."

- "We will visit and join one new group within three months."

Bob, the **Thinker:**

- "Once a month during the first six months, I will invite some Army buddies over or I will go back and see them."

- "I will visit the local humane society to learn about volunteer opportunities."

- "I will get a dog so I can become familiar with my community and meet new people while taking walks."

No matter what your style, consider setting a few goals that will enhance your transformation and at least select some these contact ideas for a plan.

Plan How to Speak to Strangers (Phases 3 & 4)

It is not always easy to speak to strangers. Your comfort level might be, "I dread meeting new people" or at the other end, your comfort level is, "I'm glad for the opportunity!" The key is to plan for this essential step because any reluctance needs to be overcome if you want to find new friends, companion, and business folks.

How to Meet New People

Some of the following suggestions should help you plan for meeting people, regardless of your comfort level doing so.

Contact Early and Often (Phases 3 & 4)

Even before you move, start making contacts to lay the groundwork for forming new relationships.

Email is an easy way to reach out to new people. If this is a referral, state on the subject line the name of the person who gave you this referral. List their name one more time in the body of your message.

Develop a short introduction with some details about who you are, your work, interests, and hobbies. Ask some questions so your new contact has a reason to reply. Or offer to reach out to them. One of my examples is shown below.

Example Email

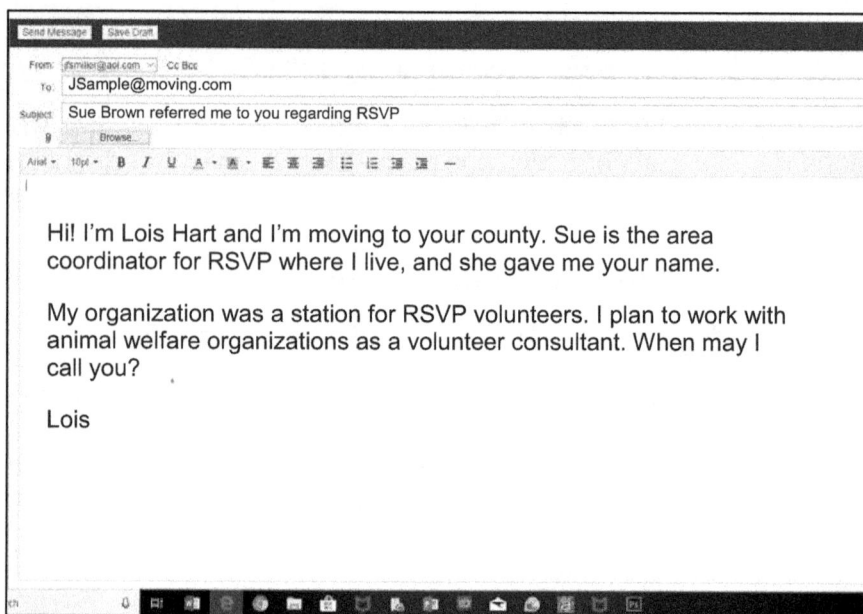

*RSVP (Retired and Senior Volunteer Program)

Do this early and expect results. Keep notes. If you take an advance trip, make plans to meet some of these people.

Don't be offended if some of these contacts don't respond. With today's busy pace and the proliferation of emails, yours may get ignored. You will need to be patient and persistent to get the attention of some people. If you had no luck making contact before you move, call them once you've landed in the new location.

Make a Contact Card (Phases 3 & 4)

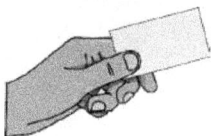

There is some degree of urgency to doing this task. As an example, once when we moved to a new state, I only had business cards from Colorado. I was busy settling in and did not realize how unprepared I was without a new card.

When I would meet someone I wanted to re-connect with later on, I would have to dig around for paper and pen. During one of my most productive days of meeting people, I only had a napkin to write on! I knew I had to do something—and soon.

Take it from me, as soon as your phone number and email address are confirmed, decide which of the following two types of cards work best for you.

1. Prepare a traditional business/personal card with your contact information. Even if you have a business card, you should consider making a personal one too. Many print shops, local and on the Internet, provide ready-made logos for cards. Choose a paper that allows you to write in pen or pencil. Glossy paper doesn't work for taking notes.

2. Consider a creative alternative with a Meet and Greet card. I created a 5" by 8" card that told more about us beyond the usual contact details. As you will see in this example, we listed our joint interests and then described some individual interests plus some of our professional background. I added a closing line that connects back to them.

I highly recommend this kind of personal card. Every time I passed one out, we got raving reviews. It definitely upped the possibility that we would hear from them. Successful networkers always carry their cards wherever they go. Never leave home without them!

A sample contact card is shown on the following page.

Lois and **Arn Hart** are on a new voyage from Colorado to our current port-of-call and homestead:

Lake View Drive
Polson, Montana

Contact us at:
100-883-8888
harts@gmail.net

We enjoy reading, music,
history, animals, sailing, and exploring new places.

Lois gardens, landscapes, arranges and presses flowers, and makes cards. Lois taught school and trained adults. She heads a non-profit to disseminate leadership models that will enhance leaders. She is currently writing a book on Celebrations at Work.

Arn reads philosophy and history plus enjoys baseball and even playing baseball simulations. He was a Radar Navigator with Air Force SAC, a teacher, and an investment broker.

**We enjoyed meeting you and want to hear
more of your story!**

Successful networkers always carry their cards wherever they go. Never leave home without them! However, in 2017, something interesting happened to me when I was at a professional association meeting. I met a man who is Generation Z. Do you know the classifications of generations? He was young (to me). When we started to really interact, I found it most interesting and wanted to talk further with him. I offered him my card and requested his. He laughed and said, "No one uses cards any more—just tell me your email and I'll put it in my phone." Wow—was I surprised! He didn't even want my phone number! This interaction taught me that I needed to remain flexible if I wanted to meet many kinds of people.

Organize Your Contacts (Phases 3 & 4)

With some effort, you will meet new people. With more effort, you will quickly get even more contacts. No matter how many you have, keep track of your contacts.

A systematic Thinker and Sensor will create organized methods to keep track of the cards, slips of paper, and other notations. Feelers and Intuitors may be less organized but will discover their own way of handling these new contacts.

It helps to at least put the contact information in the same place. When you return home or to your office, take out the cards or papers from your wallet, purse, or car, and put them in your chosen space to store.

An additional way of organizing your contacts is into categories based on your goals. For instance, if your goal is to learn to play golf, to find volunteer opportunities, or find a book club, put contacts in the appropriate category.

Move In (Phase 4)

Regardless of how far away you move, whether you hire a mover or do it yourself, no matter what your dominant style is, remember that relaunching your life in a new location is very tiring and stressful.

The physical act of unpacking, organizing, arranging, and setting up is daunting. Suddenly, you are alone at home without the friends and family you left behind.

- Review suggestions made in Chapter 3 about handling stress.
- Get as much sleep as possible.
- Take a walk everyday if only for only ten minutes.
- Be realistic about how much you can handle.
- Hire help.

- Don't rush the process of re-launching your life.
- Believe/visualize that you will find just the right people to add to your life!

Keep your expectations realistic. It will take time to find people with whom you want a significant relationship. As an employee or if you own a business, or are a full-time student, you likely work long hours. You can't just drop working to meet new people.

Set realistic goals and be selective about which methods or ideas you choose to implement. Use networking skills first within your business, school, or organization and later on, to expand your networking circle outside of work.

Expect the Unexpected (Phase 4)

You may find new friends in unlikely, yet everyday places. Some examples include:

- Wandering through the Botanic Gardens
- At a coffee shop counter
- In line for groceries or at the bank
- Dropping off items at the recycling center
- Waiting for your car at a quick lube
- Copying a report
- In an exercise class
- Buying food at the school's bake sale
- Attending local football or baseball games
- Sharing a table in the company cafeteria
- Browsing for books
- Waiting in line to buy tickets at the local theater
- Walking the dog

The possibilities are endless!

You May Not Know (Phase 4)

When we make assumptions, we are often disappointed or sorry because later on, we find out the truth or reality behind our assumptions. Be very careful when you make assumptions about people or organizations in your new location.

When Ted moved into his new house, the people next door never came over. By the fourth week, he made the assumption that they were unfriendly! Boy, was he ever wrong! When an old dog wandered into his yard, he went to this supposedly "unfriendly" neighbor. It was their dog and they were very grateful he came over. Quickly he discovered they were very busy people and that was why they had not made the effort to come by and introduce themselves.

Pure Luck! (Phase 4)

There will be some occasions when you meet new people and can only call it pure luck. Chance encounters of the good kind can be magical.

Near our new home, we had a park where we took our lunch and our dog. During one picnic, I was eating a piece of bread and swallowed it too quickly. I coughed and coughed. This voice out of nowhere calls out, "Are you all right?" We answered, "Yes, and thanks!" Within three minutes this friendly woman showed up with a bottle of water. We were so touched that we invited her to sit down with us. Fifteen minutes later, we went back to her home nearby to meet her husband. We stayed for two hours and made plans to meet again. These people became future Keepers of ours. This chance encounter was pure luck!

Mark the Calendar and Join Up! (Phase 4)

Review the groups, clubs or associations you selected as prospects. Mark on your calendar when the most interesting ones will be meeting.

Even if you are not fully settled or fully unpacked, you want to take a break from your work to set up your new space. Don't be hard on yourself. Listen to what your head and your heart say. Call or email each organization that you want to visit. Plan to attend as soon you can in the near future.

Select one to join. Sign up to help with a special event or on a committee. This is another way to meet people who are new to your circle.

Volunteer (Phase 4)

In every community, and especially in these times when volunteerism is at an all-time low, there are many places where you can volunteer and also meet lots of new people. As a newcomer, you could test the waters without making a long-term commitment. Select the volunteer job that will most likely help you expand your network.

- Serve as a greeter at your church or faith community.
- Help with a fundraising event for the Humane Society or ASPCA.
- Assist the library with their campaign for increased tax revenue.
- Use your computer skills to help the history museum upgrade their records of donors and members.
- Volunteer with a mentoring program at the local Boys and Girls Club, or if they do not have one, help set one up.
- Offer to help paint the Senior Center.
- Sell raffle tickets at your workplace.
- Sign up to staff a booth at a community fair.

Teach a Class (Phase 4)

Teaching others something you know is an excellent way to meet new people who share your interests, skills, or profession.

What are some topics you could teach others? Select the one topic or skill you either feel most passionately about or could easily prepare for teaching. Write up a short description including a snappy title and a list of specific outcomes that participants will achieve.

Check with libraries, public schools, and community colleges that offer continuing education and offer to teach a class.

Fred started teaching classes on investment strategies through the local library. He not only met some very interesting people, but several became his clients.

When I meet new people, I often mention that I am an author. I was amazed at how many people I meet who want to write a book. I eventually created a course outline and proposal on how to write and I took it to my local college.

Go Shopping! (Phase 4)

As you are unpacking in your new home, you will most likely discover items you need to buy. Typical items might be a watering can, curtains, wastebaskets, or a wheelbarrow. Perhaps you love antiques and want to find a bureau, mirror or hutch.

There are three sources to shop for your new items and all three are excellent sources to meet new people: retail stores, fairs, and garage sales.

At the retail store, strike up a conversation and mention you are new to town. Ask something about the area. For instance, at the nursery, ask about local garden clubs. At the home improvement center, ask for referrals to a handyman or plumber.

The second source for shopping and meeting potential new friends is to attend a fair, festival or show that includes vendors. As you peruse the booths, strike up conversations as described above. You may choose to follow up with some with whom you share similar interests like antiques, remodeling, crafts or decorating.

The third source for shopping are garage or tag sales. When looking for garden tools, hoses, and carts, we met one of our neighbors who lived very close by. My husband learned the man was also a veteran. The man invited him to the next American Legion meeting.

"Who else do you think I should meet?" (Phase 4)

When you meet new people in your new location, remember to ask, "Who else do you think I should meet?" After you meet the people they referred you to, call to thank the person who gave the recommendation to you.

Ask, "What do you like best?" (Phase 4)

As you meet new people, every two weeks or so evaluate them relative to what kinds of people you want in your life. This way you can decide who are the most promising Keepers. However, you won't know who will meet your needs best if you don't follow-up with them.

Keep in mind that they already have a life in this location and probably a full calendar of activities, obligations, friends, and colleagues. You don't have a life yet in this location. They don't wake up thinking, "Today I'm going to make the effort meet one new person." You need to be proactive and wake up thinking that. Reach out and find out more about them.

After meeting potential Keepers, send them an email or card indicating how much you enjoyed meeting them. Give them your contact information again. Indicate if you are either plan-ning to call them or you are waiting to hear details about the group in which they are involved.

If two weeks pass, call them. They might feel somewhat guilty about not calling you, so reassure them you do understand. Then try to get an appointment to meet them over coffee or a meal or perhaps to attend their group's next meeting.

Be patient, but persistent. After you know enough people, try the following ideas.

Form Your Own Club

Why not form your own club, group, or network? Here are some ideas:

- You love to read so form a Book Club. Ask your new acquaintances if they also like this idea.

- You are an environmentalist with concerns about land use in this new location. Start an Issues Club. Attend community and governmental meetings around these two issues. Observe what people say at these meetings and then go introduce yourself. You probably could find three other people quickly who share your views.

- Form a Presidents' Club of other entrepreneurs. You can narrow membership down to a certain age group or years in business, or perhaps to people in the same profession or industry.

Host a Coffee Klatch, Breakfast Club, or Brown-Bag Lunch

Even busy people need to eat, so turn that need into a short event so you can follow up with certain people. Select people and invite them to:

- A half hour Coffee Klatch in your office or at the local café.

- An hour continental breakfast. Structure the conversation so everyone does some sharing and you will get to know them better.

- A Brown Bag Lunch perhaps in a park or in company conference room.

Host Your Own Party

WELCOME!
Come and join in!

After your home is settled, hold a *Welcome Party*. Invite some new friends. Ask each of them to invite one other person to your party; someone they think you would like to meet.

Here is a fun get acquainted activity that Jim used at his own party. When people arrived, he asked each of his friends to write their guest's name on the tag and why they think Jim will enjoy them.

Hi! I'm Sara.

Jim loves to fish and knows
the best fishing holes.

If Jim is interested, he asks Sara to write down her contact information and when she might be going fishing next. As people mix and mingle, quite a few people will make new connections, not just Jim.

How Long Will It Take?

How long will it take before you start getting phone calls and have a few new friends? When I surveyed people who moved, almost everyone said that it took about four to six months.

Of course, this depends on how much you put into making this happen. The amount of time you have to devote will also depend on your work and home responsibilities. It will also depend on how well you have let go of your previous home and the people there, so you can make room for new people.

This is why it is smart to be realistic with your goals. Instead of calling back three new contacts, call the best one. Instead of trying to visit one new organization, church, group or club every two weeks, make your goal to visit one a month.

It's time to re-launch your life in a new location.

Chapter 8

Rejoice in Your Relationships

Upon Reflection

My latest moving journey has ended in a most gratifying manner, as I hope it will for you too. Reflection on the experience helps us analyze what worked and what didn't, so we learn from it.

In the Preface, I outlined all the moves I've made. Each was unique and the set of circumstances differed. Upon reflection on my many journeys, I concluded that some circumstances made it easier to launch new meaningful relationships and some were more challenging.

The circumstances for every move were unique. I think that some required a steeper climb to build new relationships. Consider a few typical circumstances:

1. Are you a student, employed or retired?

   Students benefit from meeting new people in classes or at the student union.

   Employed people share the organizational mission and in their own department they share similar skills. This facilitates starting new collegial relationships.

   Retired people are free of the daily obligations they faced when either running their own business or working for others. They have time to explore recreational activities and volunteer opportunities where they meet people with common interests.

2. Will you be moving to a large city or small town?

   For me the most challenging circumstances were moving into a large city or metropolitan area because the sheer number of people was overwhelming. In a smaller town or city, I made friends more easily partly because we lived near to one another and easily ran into each other around town.

3. Will there be a short or long distance between where you live now and where you are going?

   It was definitely harder to say goodbye to friends and colleagues when 1,000 miles separated us! Clearly, we wouldn't see each other much and I had to creatively find ways to maintain the relationships.

   Our latest move was to an adjoining city with about 10 miles between their borders and where we were. To us this didn't feel too far to go to the previous location to visit folks, attend meetings, or go to events.

   How far feels too far to you? Recently one friend who moved 20 minutes away from good friends said one friend bemoaned the move because of the distance.

4. Will the size of the organization you will work in or you chose to join affect making new relationships?

   The larger organization gives people more choices but the size could also mean you recognize few people in a large company cafeteria or at coffee hour after church.

   People who are more introverted may likely find large numbers uncomfortable.

   The size isn't an impediment for an enthusiast. In large organizations, I joined smaller groups, like a committee or task force, that made potential bonding easier.

Celebrate Saying Goodbye and Saying Hello

Close your eyes and reflect on this wonderful journey you have been on! Visualize where you used to live. Visualize your Keepers smiling and waving goodbye to you. Visualize your new location and some of your new friends and colleagues as they hold out welcoming arms to you.

Celebrate the transition of moving and how you have transformed your life.

Look Back and Rejoice!

You have covered a lot of territory on this moving journey. No matter how far away you moved, the reasons you moved, nor what methods or ideas you used, you have changed during this transition.

Look back now at your journey and answer the following questions:

My Moving Journey

What did you learn most about on this journey?

_____

_____

_____

_____

_____

_____

_____

_____

_____

_____

_____

Moving? Saying Goodbye and Saying Hello!

What have you learned about the four phases of moving?

_____

_____

_____

_____

_____

_____

_____

Did you mostly rely on your primary moving style or did you tap into all four styles?

_____

_____

_____

_____

_____

_____

_____

How many Keepers did you retain in the first six months? After a year?

_____

_____

_____

_____

_____

_____

_____

Rejoice in Your Relationships

What would you do differently to select and stay in touch with your Keepers?

_____

_____

_____

_____

_____

_____

_____

What worked best for you to meet new people in your new location? Consider the polarities of circumstances discussed above.

_____

_____

_____

_____

_____

_____

_____

_____

_____

_____

_____

_____

_____

What additional ideas did you try to build your new network?

_____

_____

_____

_____

_____

_____

_____

_____

_____

_____

_____

_____

How did you initially feel about moving? Did your attitude change for the better by the end of the transition?

_____

_____

_____

_____

_____

_____

_____

_____

_____

_____

_____

_____

In what ways did the moving process transform you?

_____

_____

_____

_____

_____

_____

_____

_____

_____

_____

_____

_____

Five Essential Relationship Keys

Remember five essential relationship keys for your relocation:

Review your moving style, phases of moving, and goals
Retain and **Relish** your Keepers
Release what holds you back from moving on
Re-Launch your new life with **Rich Relationships**
Rejoice in your transformation

Relationships are key in your life wherever you move!

R   Remember, moving is just one more stage in the journey of life.

E   Expand your Expectations—but also be realistic.

L   Learn from the experiences of others.

A   Attitude is everything—shift yours to positive!

T   Take your Keepers with you.

I   Involve others in helping you at all phases of the transition.

O   Openness and flexibility are important. Consider your Options.

N   Networking is the key to establishing new relationships.

S   Sad feelings often precede happy feelings.

H   Healthy habits are good—eat right, get sleep, and exercise.

I   Innovation and creativity can help to expand your options.

P   Planning makes the difference when you move out and on.

S   Success! Pack your Suitcase because this move will be successful!

Bon Voyage!

At this juncture in the road, you and I need to say "au revoir" but not "good-bye". You have used the ideas, models, and stories in this book to enhance your moving experience.

I always enjoy getting feedback from people who read any of my books.

Send me an email at loisbhart@comcast.net

www.ingramcontent.com/pod-product-compliance
Lightning Source LLC
Chambersburg PA
CBHW052119090426

42741CB00009B/1879